With All Your Mind

Autism and the Church

Erin Burnett

First published in 2022

Copyright © 2022 Erin Burnett

Cover design and typesetting: Averill Buchanan

To Ben.
This book would not have been possible without
your support, humour and theological insights.

Contents

Introduction

This booklet is aimed at anyone with an interest in autism and the Christian faith. Perhaps you are an autistic person seeking deeper self-understanding, just like me. Or maybe you are a parent or friend of an autistic person and you want a glimpse into their world. Or you might be a church leader who desires to integrate autistic people into your congregation. Regardless of who you are, I hope you find *With All Your Mind* useful. This booklet aims to give the reader a good understanding of what autism is, some ideas for making your church welcoming for autistic people, and also an exploration of how autistic people may view the Christian faith in a way that differs from the norm.

I suppose I should introduce myself before we go any further. My name is Erin Burnett, and I will be your guide into the weird and wonderful world of autism. I was diagnosed when I was eighteen after many years of not 'fitting in'. It is as if there is an invisible wall between me and other people. They are *there*, and I am *here*. I understand them to a certain degree, for they are humans just like me, with bodies and minds and opinions and actions. Yet they often act in ways that are utterly perplexing. Others are an enigma to me, a seemingly unsolvable puzzle that I attempt to piece together. My inner conflict comes from two desires, equally strong and completely opposing. One is a desire to live in my own world, to withdraw and be at peace, yet the other is a desire for warmth, attention and friendship.

I present like a lot of autistic adults in that I am highly capable in some areas and not so much in others. I have a first-class university degree, yet I struggle to get ready in the morning. I have a photographic memory when it comes to books, but I struggle to remember people's names. I am also a Christian. Like many in Northern Ireland, I was raised in a Christian home and I developed a deeper interest in the faith as I got older. The church offered a sense of belonging and community when I was feeling isolated. My favourite verse is John 15:15, when Jesus says 'I have called you friends'. This is a profoundly meaningful teaching for someone who is lonely and seeking connection, both with God and other people. I have been all over the theological spectrum in my time and I now feel spiritually at home in the Anglican tradition, although I can appreciate the beauty of many different forms of Christian expression.

My interest in Christianity led me to attend theological college, where I developed a more mature understanding of the faith. I also discovered a love for practical theology, the study of how lofty theological ideas can have real-life impact. I conducted research on how churches can be more welcoming for autistic people, but such research is only useful if the findings can make their way from the ivory tower into the hands of ordinary Christians. That is what I hope to achieve by writing this booklet – I wish to present the latest research on autism and theology in an accessible way, devoid of the esoteric and frankly dull language of academia (sincerest apologies to my professors for that comment).

Most people are impacted by autism in some way; even if you are not autistic yourself, you probably have family and friends who are on the spectrum. Everybody benefits when we strive to create a world where different ways of thinking are accommodated, particularly in a church context. It brings us one step closer to the Apostle Paul's vision for church articulated in 1 Corinthians 12, whereby each individual plays a unique and valuable part in the body of Christ.

I must make it clear that I do not speak on behalf of all autistic people. No one does. As the NHS points out on its website, 'Autism is a spectrum. This means everybody with autism is different'.[1] Nevertheless, I hope what I write will resonate with many people. If you are unsure if certain aspects apply to an autistic person in your life, ask them! Even if they do not communicate verbally, many autistic people can still communicate using assistive technologies. In cases where the individual cannot communicate, the next best thing is to talk to the person who knows them best, usually a parent. It is vitally important that autistic people are given agency over how they are treated rather than being shoved into a one-size-fits-all approach.

In this booklet I will answer four key questions:

- What is autism?
- What can churches do to be more welcoming of autistic people?
- How do autistic people approach spirituality?
- Are there any aspects of Christianity that autistic people may find difficult?

I do not intend this booklet to be a prescriptive textbook; rather, it should be a conversation starter. There will be questions for reflection at the end of each section, which can be mulled over individually or discussed in a group setting.

Without further ado, let's start by defining exactly what autism is.

CHAPTER 1
Defining Autism

It is very difficult to precisely define autism, as it is a spectrum condition that manifests differently for each person. The stereotypical image of autism is that of a child, typically male, trapped in their own world and unable to communicate. This is only one of many ways in which autistic people present. The autism spectrum can range from someone who is slightly quirky to someone with profound disability who requires 24/7 care, and every degree in between. The simplest way to define autism is that it is a neurobiological condition which affects how a person interprets and interacts with the world; autistic people are 'different, not less' as Temple Grandin often says.[2] Autism is not in itself a mental illness or a learning disability, although autistic people often have co-occurring mental and physical health issues.

Before we can delve into issues surrounding autism and the church, we first need to go over the basics. What are the characteristics of autism? Is autism on the rise? Are there any public figures who are autistic? This chapter will answer these questions and more.

Characteristics of Autism

Most discussions about autism focus only on deficits and paint a rather bleak picture of the condition. It is important to highlight the positive aspects of autism as well as being realistic about the challenges. The following characteristics are not intended to be an exhaustive list of diagnostic criteria. They are common traits amongst autistic people, and you may recognise some of them in yourself or your loved ones. I include examples of how these traits manifest in my life, but I do not claim that my experience applies to all autistic people. To quote Dr Stephen Shore, 'If you've met one person with autism, you've met one person with autism.'[3] We're not all the same! Just like anyone else, autistic people are made in the image of God and have unique personalities with their own strengths and weaknesses. Listening to the individual is key: if you are not sure if some of these characteristics apply to an autistic person in your life, ask them. Or, if they cannot communicate for themselves, ask the person who knows them best.

Social Difficulties

Difficulty with socialising is perhaps the most significant characteristic of autism. Socialising does not come naturally to us in the way it does to neurotypical people; we are baffled by the rules of conversation that come instinctively to others. It's like suddenly finding yourself surrounded by people who speak a different language – everyone around you knows how to communicate with each other, but you are completely lost. Both verbal and non-verbal forms of communication are affected. Many autistic people develop speech later than average, and some remain non-verbal. For those of us who can speak, it can be difficult to get the balance between give and take in a conversation – some autistic people rarely speak, whereas others never stop speaking. Language devices such as metaphor and sarcasm can be difficult for literal-minded people to interpret; turns out that if someone says you have a heart of gold (or stone!) they do not mean your heart is comprised of a substance other than human flesh. Interestingly, sarcasm is one thing I've personally never had a problem with – I imagine that's as a result of growing up in Northern Ireland! As for non-verbal forms of communication, it is often said that most communication takes place without words; things like body language, gestures, tone and eye contact are a vital part of communication that autistic people often struggle to interpret, which can lead to misunderstandings.

The most difficult aspect of social impairment is that most autistic people sincerely want to have friends but don't have the skills to do so. For me, this became apparent when I started secondary school. Primary school was easy. All you had to do was find other kids who liked Pokémon and instantly become friends. Once hormones kick in things become infinitely more complicated. I spent most of my teenage years dreadfully lonely, pouring myself into my studies as a distraction. My difficulties were not the result of bullying or deliberate exclusion; many girls at school made an effort to include me, but I was unable to reciprocate even though I really wanted to. My silence was taken as a lack of interest, and thus I was left to my own devices. Situations like this are why early diagnosis and autism awareness are crucial. If my autism had been picked up earlier, I could have got the support I needed much sooner.

Sensory Hypersensitivity

Sensory issues are another common characteristic of autism. Autistic people can be over- or under-sensitive to external stimuli like lights, noise, smells, taste and touch. Overstimulation can cause distress and in worst cases can cause a meltdown or shutdown. In order to cope with sensory overload, autistic people often engage in self-stimulating behaviours, otherwise known as 'stimming'. Common stims include flapping and rocking back and forth. Stimming is nothing to be concerned about as long as it is not causing further distress. Personally, I am most sensitive to sound. I am almost always wearing snazzy noise-cancelling headphones or earplugs. A professor at the theological college I attended said he would remember me as the girl with the pink headphones – I'm quite happy with that. Hypersensitivity can also be a good thing; certain stimuli can be very calming. Sensory rooms are designed with this in mind, as they contain various pieces of equipment which are scientifically proven to reduce anxiety. Sensory rooms are often found in special schools and increasingly in public venues as well, such as the Belfast Christmas Market. Some churches have them, which is an immense blessing for autistic people and their families.

Intense Interests

Autistic people tend to have intense and extremely focused interests. Anything under the sun – or even the sun itself – can become an interest. Intense interests can come and go, and some may be lifelong. Interests can bring great joy to autistic people and can also help with socialisation if they can connect with other people with the same interest. If you want to connect with an autistic person in your life, a great place to start is by learning a little about their interests and chatting to them about what they like. Oftentimes there isn't any clear reason why someone has a particular interest. For instance, my most intense interest is rabbits, despite the fact that I have never owned a rabbit. I just think they're the best. Some interests can be channelled into a very successful career. For instance, Stephen Shore is an autistic man whose childhood interest was taking watches apart. His parents encouraged his interest and gave him other objects to disassemble. Upon reaching adulthood he became a bicycle mechanic, using the skills he had developed through pursuing his special interest. He is now a professor of special education.

Attention to Detail

Multiple scientific papers have demonstrated that autistic people have a greater than average attention to detail and an ability to recognise patterns. *Monotropism* is the fancy psychological term for this characteristic; monotropic minds can focus intently on one thing at a time, oblivious to what is occurring outside their focus. Autistic people tend to have an all-or-nothing approach to what they do – if they find something they enjoy and are good at, they can be absorbed in it for hours. This is a very useful skill to have in academia or STEM fields, and many autistic people end up in computer-related careers for this reason.

Like many traits related to autism, attention to detail has both positives and negatives. Intense focus on one thing means we can be quite poor at multitasking. Tasks like cooking can be difficult, as it involves focussing on many different things at once. Even a basic recipe like beans on toast involves several concurrent tasks: open the tin, heat the beans, toast the bread... it can be a lot to keep track of. For this reason, home help can be very beneficial to help autistic people with the tasks of daily living, and it can enable them to live semi-independently.

Enhanced Memory

Memory also tends to be enhanced, although it can be quite selective – we're very good at remembering information and facts, particularly if it's related to a special interest, but remembering people's names and faces can be tricky. I can ruin any party I attend by naming all 151 original Pokémon, but please don't be offended if I forget your name. Some autistic people have eidetic (photographic) memory, meaning they can recall images with exceptional detail. If you want to see eidetic memory in action, check out videos of Stephen Wiltshire at work. He is an autistic man who draws amazingly detailed cityscapes from memory, earning him the nickname of 'human camera'.

A small subsection of autistic people have *savant syndrome*, which is when someone who is intellectually disabled demonstrates extraordinary ability in one area. *Rain Man* is the enduring stereotype for this kind of autism, a film in which Dustin Hoffman plays an autistic adult with extraordinary mathematical ability (Hoffman's character in *Rain Man* was based upon a real-life savant named Kim Peek, who had memorised the contents of 12,000 books). However, this only applies to a very small percentage of autistic people, and many parents of autistic children with high support needs are tired of being asked if their child has a special talent. Autism is a spectrum; some autistic people are savant-level geniuses, some are profoundly impaired, and most are somewhere in the middle.

Is Autism on the Rise?

It may seem that autism is a modern phenomenon, but it has been around for much longer than most people realise. Autism was not formally diagnosed until 1943, but there are many historical figures who would likely meet today's diagnostic criteria. For instance, whenever I read Hans Christian Andersen's autobiography *The Fairy Tale of My Life* (1871), it portrayed a man who was highly intelligent but also a social outcast. Much of what he wrote resonated with me.[4] One of his most well-known fairy tales, *The Ugly Duckling*, was based upon his experiences of never fitting in. I am not the only person to suspect Andersen was on the spectrum; Michael Fitzgerald, an Irish professor who specialises in autism, expresses the same opinion in his book about autism and creativity.[5] Although it is impossible to diagnose retrospectively, it is undeniable that autism existed long before it was formally identified.

It is clear that autism *diagnoses* are certainly on the rise. In Northern Ireland alone, the Department of Health's most recent statistics estimate that 4.5% of school-aged children are autistic, up from 1.2% in 2008.[6] This increase could be due to increased awareness and better diagnostic services rather than an increase in prevalence. In the past, autistic people were often institutionalised, so it is possible that autism was just as prevalent then as it is now, but it was more hidden from society. It's still unknown exactly what causes autism, so there is no definite answer to why diagnoses are going up. It's likely due to a combination of genetic, environmental and social factors.

Increased awareness of autism in women and girls has also contributed to the overall increase in diagnoses. Officially, autistic boys outnumber autistic girls 10 to 1, but this is because girls are woefully undiagnosed. Girls can be autistic too, but most of the early research on autism was based on male children; it is only in recent years that research has been done on how autism presents differently in girls. Girls are less likely to 'act out' and are more adept at masking (faking 'normal' behaviour in order to fit in). Many women and girls end up being treated for secondary conditions like obsessive-compulsive disorder, anxiety and depression, without ever getting to the root cause of their difficulties. Indeed, I once had a well-meaning therapist tell me that my loneliness would be solved if I just talked to other girls at school – if it was that easy, I wouldn't have been in therapy! If the public image of autism remains that of a young male child, it is no wonder that therapists miss the signs of autism in other demographics.

The Language Debate

There is much debate over the language that should be used when talking about autism. People disagree on whether we should use identity-first (autistic person) or person-first phrasing (person with autism). There are positives to each approach. Identity-first language conveys that autism is a core part of someone's identity and not something to be ashamed of. Person-first language, on the other hand, recognises that autism is just one of many things that make up an individual's identity. I prefer person-first phrasing because I am an individual first and foremost. Autism is certainly part of my identity, but it does not define me. However, opinion polls demonstrate that I am in the minority on this one, so I shall use identity-first language throughout this booklet.[7] Hurrah for democracy. Discourse between the two 'sides' can get rather heated, particularly on internet comment sections. As

Christians, I hope we can have the charity and understanding required to respect those who disagree with our opinions on such matters. The Apostle Paul was no stranger to debate and division within the communities he corresponded with, and his advice in his letter to the Romans is as relevant today as it was two thousand years ago: 'If possible, so far as it depends on you, live peaceably with all' (Romans 12:18).

Another shift in language over recent years has been the drift away from using the term 'Asperger's syndrome'. The Asperger's syndrome diagnosis referred to people who have many autistic traits, but without language delay or intellectual disability. The term was removed from American diagnostic manuals in 2013 and is slowly being phased out in the UK; those who previously would have had this diagnosis are now considered to be part of the broader autism spectrum. However, it remains true that those of us who previously would have qualified for a diagnosis of Asperger's present very differently from those with so-called 'classic autism', and we need some way of referring to our differences in order to get the right support. I quite like using the terms 'high support needs' and 'low support needs' as a sensitive yet accurate way to refer to the different support requirements across the spectrum.

Disorder, Disability or Difference?

Another debate within the autism community is how autism should be categorised: is it a disorder, a disability or a benign difference? When it comes to autism, there are two equal yet opposite erroneous ways of looking at the condition. Some view autism as a terrible disorder that should be eradicated at all costs, whereas others view it as a gift that should always be celebrated. Both positions lack nuance and fail to consider the full range of the autism spectrum. For some people, autism is indeed a gift – it enables them to see the world differently and achieve wonderful things. For others, their autism is of such severity that it causes them suffering on a daily basis. Most autistic people are somewhere in the middle. I cringe when I read sentences like 'all autistic people think…' or 'all autistic people are…'. There is no 'all' when it comes to autism; everyone presents differently. I have spoken to many parents of autistic people who are afraid to admit their struggles in case they are accused of not fully accepting their children. It is possible to love your child with every fibre of your being while admitting sometimes life with autism is hard. Faith-based communities in particular should be safe spaces where autistic people and their carers can speak candidly about their experiences without facing criticism or condemnation for their views.

One of my favourite autism bloggers is Eileen Lamb, a French woman who runs a website named The Autism Café. I appreciate her balanced take on autism, acknowledging both its joys and its challenges. Lamb speaks from personal experience – both she and her son are on the spectrum. She writes:

> I wish we could find a middle ground between 'autism is a superpower' and 'autism is the end of the world'. Many believe we shouldn't use severity levels anymore and that autism is a difference, not a disability. I believe there's a way to be an autism advocate without losing sight of how severely (and sometimes negatively) many autistic people are affected. I believe the answer is somewhere in the middle. We need to keep in mind how broad the spectrum is. There are people on both ends of it, and some somewhere in the middle too, with levels of functioning varying drastically from one person to another, and one day to the next too.[8]

To return to the question posed at the beginning of this section, is autism a disorder, disability or difference? All of the above! When I'm acing exams due to my photographic memory, my autism is a gift. When I was crushingly lonely during adolescence, my autism was a disorder. Much like the language debate, we should allow individuals to decide how they want to view their own autism. It's worth pointing out that calling something a disability or a disorder is not inherently negative. It is simply a descriptor which acknowledges the challenges and allows people to access the support they require. Being disabled doesn't make someone 'less than' – we are all made in the image of God and have inherent worth.

Autistic Role Models

It is important for autistic people and their families to have positive examples of autistic people who are living happy and fulfilled lives to help combat negative stereotypes and to give people hope for their future. These could be celebrities or people in your personal life. The following is a list of my autistic role models:

Temple Grandin is perhaps the most famous autistic person alive today. She grew up in the 1950s, a time when autism was practically unheard of, especially in girls. She didn't speak until she was three and a half and doctors recommended she be institutionalised. Thankfully, her mother refused to give up on her and encouraged her to pursue her interests. Grandin was able to channel her interest in animal welfare and she designed equipment that reduces stress for livestock. Today 50% of cattle farms in the USA use equipment she designed. Grandin's story is a wonderful example of what can happen when autistic people are given the freedom to think outside the box. On top of her distinguished career in animal welfare, she has also published numerous books on autism and regularly speaks at conferences.

Lamar Hardwick is a Christian minister who refers to himself as 'The Autism Pastor'. Throughout his adult life he silently struggled with social anxiety and sensory issues, but that didn't stop him obtaining a PhD in ministry and serving as a youth leader, chaplain and minister. He wasn't diagnosed with autism until he was thirty-six. Getting a diagnosis was helpful for Hardwick: 'it has helped me to better understand how my brain works and how to best use my gifts and skills. It has also given me the freedom to focus on my strengths instead of my weaknesses'.[9] As well as being a preacher, he has written two bestselling books on disability inclusion in the·church: *I Am Strong: The Life and Journey of an Autistic Pastor* and *Disability and the Church*.[10] These books are invaluable for any autistic person who feels called to ministry. Hardwick also offers one-to-one mentoring for autistic teenagers and young adults.

Anne Hegerty is best known as 'the Governess' from ITV's *The Chase*. Enhanced memory and a passion for knowledge are common traits of autism, and these traits certainly come in handy when you answer quiz questions for a living. Similar to Hardwick, Hegerty wasn't diagnosed until later in life, when she was forty-five. She had always struggled with socialising and multitasking, and it wasn't until she saw a documentary about autistic children that she realised she was on the spectrum herself. She made headlines when she openly discussed living with autism on *I'm A Celebrity... Get Me Out*

Of Here! She received an outpouring of support, including a letter from an eleven-year-old autistic boy: 'Watching you makes me see that other people can have autism too and maybe I can have a cool job like you when I am older.'[11]

Carly Fleischmann is a talk-show host with more than three million followers. Unlike the previous people I mentioned, Fleischmann is non-verbal, meaning she cannot speak. However, just because someone cannot speak doesn't mean they have nothing to say! Fleischmann couldn't communicate at all until she was ten when her life was changed forever thanks to assistive technology. She uses a tablet with text-to-speech software that enables her to express her thoughts. She has appeared on major American talk shows such as *The Ellen DeGeneres Show* and *The Late Show with Stephen Colbert*, and she has her own show called *Speechless with Carly Fleischmann*. Fleischmann is inspiring autistic people across the world to express themselves in their own unique way – and she's only twenty-six years old!

I could list many more inspiring people, but that would take up the whole book. All of these people have one thing in common: their lives have been difficult at times, and they have had to overcome many obstacles, but they have been able to utilise the many strengths their autism gives them. Of course, not all autistic people are capable of holding down full-time jobs like the people mentioned above, and that's fine! A person's worth is not measured by their accomplishments. Don't judge a fish by its ability to climb a tree – celebrate each and every step, no matter how mundane it is.

Now that we have explored what autism is, it is time to move on to what you came here for: autism and the church.

The following chapters will explore how churches can be more welcoming to autistic people, and I will also explore how autistic people relate to God. By listening to the perspectives of those who see the world differently, churches will discover fresh ways of looking at timeless theological truths.

Questions for Reflection

- What is your personal experience of autism?
- Which of the traits listed resonate with you and/ or your loved one?
- Are there any traits not listed that are worth mentioning?
- Do you have any autistic role models?

CHAPTER 2
Autism and the Church

The National Autistic Society estimates 1 in 100 people in the UK are autistic – a figure likely to increase as diagnostic services improve.[12] It is therefore statistically likely that any given church will have at least one autistic person in their congregation. Churches have both a theological and legal obligation to remove obstacles that may prevent an autistic person from fully participating in a church community: theological because churches should follow the example of Jesus, who reached out to those who were ostracised from society, and legal because the Autism Act (NI) 2013 requires all organisations to make 'reasonable adjustments' for autistic people (similar legislation exists in other UK regions).[13] This chapter will examine what the Bible can teach us about inclusion and will also give some practical tips for making churches more welcoming to all.

1 Corinthians 12: 14–27
A Church of Many Parts

Even so the body is not made up of one part but of many.

Now if the foot should say, 'Because I am not a hand, I do not belong to the body,' it would not for that reason stop being part of the body. And if the ear should say, 'Because I am not an eye, I do not belong to the body,' it would not for that reason stop being part of the body.

If the whole body were an eye, where would the sense of hearing be? If the whole body were an ear, where would the sense of smell be? *But in fact God has placed the parts in the body, every one of them, just as he wanted them to be.* If they were all one part, where would the body be? As it is, there are many parts, but one body.

The eye cannot say to the hand, 'I don't need you!' And the head cannot say to the feet, 'I don't need you!' *On the contrary, those parts of the body that seem to be weaker are indispensable, and the parts that we think are less honourable we treat with special honour.* And the parts that are unpresentable are treated with special modesty, while our presentable parts need no special treatment.

But God has put the body together, giving greater honour to the parts that lacked it, so that there should be no division in the body, but that its parts should have equal concern for each other. If one part suffers, every part suffers with it; if one part is honoured, every part rejoices with it.

Now you are the body of Christ, and each one of you is a part of it.

This is one of my favourite passages of scripture. It teaches us that every person who is part of the body of Christ is deserving of honour because they are made in the image of God. Lamar Hardwick, the autistic pastor mentioned in chapter one, has written about this passage in detail. He says that autistic people may be viewed as 'weaker', yet according to this passage they are 'indispensable'. Our society judges people based on how much money they have, how productive they are and how they look – as a result, autistic people often have poor self-esteem and may feel 'less than' due to their differences. The church can be a prophetic witness in such a society by providing an environment where people of all abilities can discover what their gifts may be, which in turn will benefit the wider church community. Hardwick rightfully points out that 'the point of inclusion is not just to make them whole, but to make the community whole'.[14] There are so many ways to get involved with church life – youth and children's ministry, technology, music, reading, community projects... the list is endless. Several autistic adults I know had their first taste of public speaking by reading Bible passages in church, and this gave them some much-needed confidence and a feeling that their contribution was valued. It doesn't matter how seemingly small your contribution is. Just like a human body, every part has a different function but is equally valuable in the eyes of God: 'God has put the body together, giving greater honour to the parts that lacked it' (1 Corinthians 12: 24).

Luke 14: 15–24
The Parable of the Great Banquet

When one of those at the table with him heard this, he said to Jesus, '*Blessed is the one who will eat at the feast in the Kingdom of God.*'

Jesus replied: 'A certain man was preparing a great banquet and invited many guests. At the time of the banquet he sent his servant to tell those who had been invited, "Come, for everything is now ready."

But they all alike began to make excuses. The first said, "I have just bought a field, and I must go and see it. Please excuse me."

Another said, "I have just bought five yoke of oxen, and I'm on my way to try them out. Please excuse me."

Still another said, "I just got married, so I can't come."

The servant came back and reported this to his master. *Then the owner of the house became angry and ordered his servant, "Go out quickly into the streets and alleys of the town and bring in the poor, the crippled, the blind and the lame."*

"Sir," the servant said, "what you ordered has been done, but there is still room."

Then the master told his servant, "Go out to the roads and country lanes and compel them to come

in, so that my house will be full. I tell you, not one
of those who were invited will get a taste of my
banquet."

This passage is one of Jesus' many Kingdom parables, when
he uses a story to illustrate what the Kingdom of God looks
like. The parable of the great banquet is particularly relevant
to our topic, as it deals directly with disability. Some of the
descriptors in the passage are a bit outdated, but we can
forgive an ancient document for not using contemporary
disability terminology. The point behind the parable is
timeless: if the church is serious about manifesting the
Kingdom of God 'on earth as it is in Heaven', then we must
actively invite those who wouldn't normally have a place at
the table. In preparation for writing this chapter, I chatted
to Mark Traylor, a retired church leader who had quite a few
autistic and learning disabled people in his congregation,
really bringing this parable to life. He considers the presence
of these people to be a great blessing:

> It gives people the opportunity to interact with others
> who are differently abled and who they normally would
> not come into contact with. That allows them to see the
> truly wonderful gifts that these folks have to offer. It also
> broadens their awareness that these kinds of interactions
> enrich their lives. For those who have learning disabilities
> or are in some other way different, it has helped them to
> feel confident, and to know that they can be loved and
> included in a broader community.[15]

That sounds like the Kingdom of God to me! The Kingdom
of God is not a set location on a map. Rather, the Kingdom
is manifested wherever people live Christ-like lives: 'Nor will
they say, "Look, here it is!" or "There!" for behold, the Kingdom

of God is in the midst of you' (Luke 17:21). When speaking of the Kingdom of God, theologians refer to the 'already/not yet' dichotomy; there are aspects of the Kingdom that are already present in this life, but we remain in a world full of sin and brokenness. The full manifestation of the Kingdom of God is not accessible in this life, but all Christians should strive to live in a way that gives us glimpses of what is still to come. The Kingdom of God is counter-cultural, bringing together people that would not normally mix. There will be people of different abilities, ages, nationalities and socio-economic status, all united by a love of Christ and a desire to live a life defined by love. Having a mix of ages represented in a church can be particularly beneficial for autistic people, as many find it easier to communicate with people older or younger than them rather than their peers.

Practical Advice

The above passages are just a snapshot of what the Bible has to say about inclusion – Jesus takes inclusivity very seriously! So how can we apply this to autism and the twenty-first century church? Without adjustments, church can be an unpleasant experience for people on the spectrum. I remember a time when several youth groups in my area came together for an evening service at a local church. The service was designed to appeal to a younger demographic, so it was *very, very* loud and *very, very* bright. I didn't feel like I was participating in the service because I was far too anxious and overstimulated – I spent most of the service attempting to shield my eyes and ears. I had to ask my mum to come and rescue me before I had a full-blown meltdown. Needless to say, I didn't go to any more youth services.

What sorts of adjustments can make churches more welcoming for autistic people? I did a research project at university on that very question, which gave me the opportunity to interview many autistic Christians. I asked them to describe difficulties they face when they attend church, and what adjustments would help them to feel welcome at church. What they said is so instructive for the Church.

The single most popular suggestion was providing earplugs or noise-cancelling headphones, particularly if your church has a loud and contemporary style of worship. I once attended a very lively and noisy international church in Japan, and they had a basket of earplugs you could help yourself to in the foyer of the church. It may seem like a trivial gesture, but it meant so much to me – here I am writing about it almost three years later! It is such a simple and inexpensive way to let people with hypersensitivity to sound know that they are welcome. In a similar vein, light is another thing that autistic people can be sensitive to. Fluorescent lighting can be particularly challenging because it is unnaturally bright and makes a humming sound that is extremely distracting for many autistic people. LED lighting is a good alternative, as it is less likely to cause overstimulation and is also cheaper and better for the environment – win-win.

If the worship environment is so loud and bright that the aforementioned adjustments aren't enough, another option would be to have a breakout room where the service is broadcast remotely. One of the people I interviewed attended a church where the worship was like a music concert – great for appealing to neurotypical young people, but a sensory nightmare for autistic people! The church's solution was to broadcast the service into their café area, where autistic people can participate in a quieter environment. It is not only autistic people who use the quiet room – there are many neurotypical people who also prefer quieter worship. This goes to show that when you make adjustments for one group of people, many more can benefit.

Participants also expressed a preference for a predictable order of service, and, interestingly, the people I interviewed from liturgical traditions expressed greater satisfaction with their church experiences compared to those in more contemporary churches. This is because liturgical forms of worship tend to be more predictable and ritualistic, which suits autistic people who may struggle with unpredictability and change. This doesn't mean that autistic people can't thrive in more modern styles of worship, but they may need some extra help – a possible solution is to send the person a rough outline of each week's service in advance, even if an order of service isn't something the church would normally do. For example, one of the people I interviewed was a worship leader in a very modern style of church. Being on the worship team worked very well for her, not only because she was able to use her musical talent, but also because it meant she was directly involved with the planning of services and knew exactly what was going to happen and when.

Another thing churches can do to be more welcoming of autistic people is to avoid teaching that God wants to supernaturally cure people of autism. Trying to heal autistic people in church is a very damaging practice. It gives the impression that autistic people are only welcome if they become more 'normal'. Churches can take action to improve the lives of autistic people without trying to change a fundamental part of them. Disability activists distinguish between medical and social ways of looking at disabilities like autism; the medical model views autism as a disease to be cured, whereas the social model considers how society can change in order to be more accommodating of people with disabilities. Tonya Nash, founder of the Autism Faith Network, gives some examples of how autistic people can experience healing without being 'cured' of autism: 'Someone with autism who didn't speak who learns to communicate via voice or assistive technology? That's healing to me. If someone is now able to eat a variety of foods when they once had a strong texture issue? That's healing too!'[16]

One aspect of church life that my research didn't directly address was youth and children's work, as I only interviewed people over the age of 18. I don't have the fondest memories of my time in church youth groups – I once locked myself in a toilet to avoid having to mix with others and had to be coaxed out by a long-suffering youth leader. It wasn't because anyone was unpleasant towards me. It was because everyone else seemed to socialise so effortlessly while I found it impossible, and youth groups are extremely social environments. In preparation for writing this chapter, I chatted to a few parents of autistic young people to hear what churches were doing for their children. One mother said her son could not cope with youth groups – much like me when I was his age – so the minister had agreed to set aside time each week for him to ask questions about faith and life in a much calmer environment. Another option would be to have a youth group or Sunday school specifically for autistic people, although this is easier said than done. The leaders would need appropriate training from an organisation like the National Autistic Society, and it would probably require several churches to co-operate in order to get good numbers attending. If you feel called to such an endeavour, I recommend *Leading a Special Needs*

Ministry by Amy Fenton Lee – she gives invaluable advice for doing ministry for people who are autistic and/or learning disabled.[17]

Examples of Good Practice

The following are real-life examples of Christian initiatives which aim to improve the church experience for autistic people and their families – perhaps they will inspire you to start something similar!

SNAP

Starting with an initiative close to home in Northern Ireland, SNAP (Social Networking for children with Autism and their Parents) is a group which meets weekly in Jennymount Methodist Church, North Belfast. Conventional church activities aimed at families, such as mums and tots, are often inaccessible to parents of autistic children with complex needs. Additionally, the waiting list for government-provided autism support is dreadfully long, which leaves many parents feeling isolated and alone. SNAP offers autistic children and their parents a safe space to socialise and support each other.

The Centre for the Study of Autism and Christian Community

Across the Irish Sea in Scotland, the Centre for the Study of Autism and Christian Community is a research centre at the University of Aberdeen which conducts academic research on the intersections between autism and Christian theology. Their research delves into how autism impacts our understanding of church, prayer, liturgy, music and the eucharist. The co-director of the centre, Prof. Grant Macaskill, has written an excellent book entitled *Autism and the Church: Bible, Theology, and Community*.[18] Throughout the book, Macaskill combines his personal experience of being on the spectrum with his expertise as a New Testament professor. If you are looking for something that goes much deeper than my booklet, you will enjoy this book.

Autism Faith Network

Going even further afield – across the Atlantic this time – the Autism Faith Network was founded by Tonya Nash, the mother of two autistic sons. Her boys found it difficult to attend church because of all the sensory input and unpredictability, but that changed when they found a church with a dedicated special needs ministry. It was a shame that Nash's family had to try so many different churches before they found one equipped to serve autistic people, and she vowed to do something about it. That is when the Autism Faith Network was born. The charity provides activity ideas and educational materials for use in churches and has a list of autism-friendly churches so that autistic people can find inclusive communities. The network's long-term aim is to spread autism awareness, acceptance and inclusion in faith-based communities all over the world, not just in America. If you are interested in making your church more inclusive but don't know where to start, I would definitely recommend getting in touch with them.

This chapter has demonstrated how inclusivity is a key aspect of the Kingdom of God, and making adjustments for autistic people needn't be anything dramatic or expensive – even just a basket of earplugs at the door can make all the difference.

Now that we've explored the practical elements of autism and the church, we can move on to the deeper theological questions: How do autistic people relate to God? How do they pray? Do they have a 'personal relationship with Jesus'? All these questions will be answered, and more.

Questions for Reflection

- What verses in the two Bible passages really stood out to you?
- Can you think of any other Biblical teaching about inclusion?
- Do you think your church is a welcoming place for an autistic person? If not, what adjustments could be made?

CHAPTER 3
Autism and God

The next two chapters will consider how autistic people may experience the Christian faith in a way that differs from the norm. Many autistic people find aspects of Christianity difficult and may not feel a personal connection with God. I am one such person. If I had to encapsulate my religious outlook in one sentence, I would flip the oft-cited phrase 'spiritual, but not religious' and instead say I am 'religious, but not spiritual'. I have always had a deep-seated interest in religion, and I love the traditions, community and way of life which Christianity provides. Yet I have always struggled with the supernatural aspects of the faith; I could never grasp the concept of communicating with a God 'up there' while humans were 'down here'. I bounced from church to church, all over the theological spectrum, hoping to finally achieve the 'personal relationship with Jesus' everyone else seemed to enjoy. My research revealed I am not a hopeless heretic in a state of wilful rebellion. Instead, there are neurobiological reasons which explain why a certain percentage of autistic people struggle to relate to the supernatural aspects of the faith. This chapter will explore the reasons behind this and will consider ways in which autistic people can experience the Christian faith in a way that works for them.

Is There A Link Between Autism and Atheism?

Multiple research papers have demonstrated a connection between autism and lack of belief in a supernatural deity.[19] To use a fancy theological term, autistic people are less likely to experience *sensus divinitatus*, the inexplicable feeling of God's presence. Why is this the case? Researchers have suggested several theories. Bear with me, things are going to get a bit technical here.

A 2011 study from the University of Boston examined the religious beliefs of 400 people, half of whom were autistic and half of whom were neurotypical.[20] Their results suggest autistic people are much more likely than neurotypicals to identify as atheist or agnostic, for a variety of reasons. Autistic participants tended to avoid supernaturalism, preferred logical and scientific explanations over religious metaphors and had a more rigid way of thinking. However, the researchers noted that even the atheist autistics appreciated how socially welcoming religious communities could be.

A 2012 study from the University of British Columbia found that when some autistic people talk of God, they are not thinking of a relational being, but rather a concept.[21] For instance, Temple Grandin defined God as 'the entanglement of millions of interacting particles' rather than a person.[22] In order to have a relationship with God, one must be able to empathise with God's personality traits, thoughts, moods, and ways of communicating. Autistic people have a hard enough time doing this with someone who is standing in front of them, let alone with an entity we cannot see.

Finally, a research paper from 2014 – the result of collaboration between researchers from Queen's University Belfast and Ashford University in the States – considered the role *teleological thinking* may have in people's perceptions of God.[23] To think teleologically simply means seeing a deeper meaning behind seemingly random events. The researchers interviewed twenty-seven autistic people and thirty-four neurotypical people about significant events in their life. The neurotypical people were more likely to bring God into their stories, claiming God was in control of their lives and caused events to happen according to his plan. Contrastingly, the autistic people mostly used scientific explanations and were more likely to believe 'there is no reason why; things just happen.' These findings suggest autistic people take events at face value rather than attributing them to a higher power or supernatural force, which makes it more difficult for them to believe God has a personal plan for their life.[24]

There are more studies I could mention, but you get the gist: autistic people are less likely to believe in God, and even if they do, they may struggle to have a personal relationship with God. To use myself as an example, I find a lot of modern worship difficult to relate to. I have heard people joke that some pieces of contemporary worship music sound more like a romantic love song than a hymn – Preston Sprinkle aptly calls this 'Jesus is my boyfriend theology'.[25] Connection with God is presented as something deeply emotional and personal. Don't get me wrong, I am not looking down upon people who relate to God in this way – I wish I could! However, it's hard enough relating to other people this way, let alone an entity I cannot directly interact with. Of course, this doesn't mean all autistic people are atheists – there are many who have no problem believing in a supernatural God. However, if the church is serious about including autistic people, they must be prepared to consider different ways of looking at the Christian faith that are compatible with the way some autistic people think.

A Different Way to Look at Faith

God does not change: 'Jesus Christ is the same yesterday and today and forever' (Hebrews 13:8). The same cannot be said for people – we change all the time, and that includes sometimes changing how we practice our faith. Every human is unique and will have a unique way of approaching an unchanging God. If an autistic person cannot relate to God on a personal level, how else can they honour God in their lives? I found an answer to this question while reading the works of John Shelby Spong, former bishop of Newark, who writes about Christianity in a very nuanced and modern way. I really like how Spong perceives God: 'God is not a noun that demands to be defined, God is a verb that invites us to live, to love, and to be.'[26] Whenever we act in love and live life to the full – as Jesus himself said in John 10:10 – we are experiencing God. A similar idea is echoed in 1 John 4:16: 'Whoever lives in love lives in God, and God in them.' I may not feel a supernatural connection to God, but I can still relate to God in my own way by striving to live a life defined by love.

Autistic people are naturally curious and are not afraid to ask questions others find inappropriate. I've read articles suggesting Nicodemus may have been autistic, as he came to Jesus with a very literal-minded question no one else thought to ask: 'How can a man be born when he is old?' (John 3:4). It's probably a stretch to diagnose a character based on one question, but the principle still applies: a good church community should be able to facilitate difficult conversations. One of the best Bible studies I ever attended was during a retreat with the Corrymeela Community in Ballycastle. We discussed Matthew 25:31-46, the parable of the sheep and the goats. The gist of the parable is this: on judgement day, those who will inherit eternal life are those who feed the hungry, invite the stranger, clothe the naked, look after the sick and visit the imprisoned. We all agreed this is a very good expression of religion. However, what made this Bible study so interesting is that people weren't afraid to say parts of the text made them uncomfortable, particularly the rather violent imagery used to describe the fate of the wicked. This was mind-boggling for me. At the Bible studies I usually attended, we just said what we liked about the text and how awesome it was. We never dared to ask questions. This study was different. People were open and honest. I learned it is possible to respect the Bible while still thinking critically about it – after all, if scripture is truly God-breathed it should be able to stand up to our questioning. I firmly believe everyone should consider the views of those with whom they disagree; you are unlikely to change your mind, but you will at least understand where they are coming from. Studying theology has given me the ability to consider the merits of different schools of thought while working out my own faith.

We can apply the same critical lens to the miracle stories in the Bible. One of the studies I mentioned earlier revealed autistic people are less likely to accept supernatural explanations of mysterious events, but this shouldn't prevent them from grasping the deeper meaning behind such stories.

When Jesus heals the lepers in Mark 1, he is saving them not only from the disease, but from the sin of exclusion. Once healed, they are restored to their communities. Likewise with the woman in Luke 8 who had an unspecified bleeding issue. This story is particularly significant, as women with menstrual issues were seen as super unclean and weren't allowed anywhere near the temple. Again, the woman is saved from the sin of exclusion. The miracle narratives tell us that Jesus is more powerful than the forces of sin and death that blight this world. By looking at the sort of people Jesus performed miracles for – people who were rejected by their society – we get a good sense of what he was all about. The Kingdom of God is all about saving mankind from our own selfishness by creating an inclusive community where love and justice are key. To clarify, I am not saying that Jesus' miracles didn't happen, I am simply pointing out that autistic people can still engage with the Biblical narratives regardless of how literally they view the miracle stories. To quote Richard Holloway, 'If you insist that myth has to be understood in its literal or unbroken sense, then you are in danger of excluding me from its value altogether, because I am unable to submit to your particular version of it.'[27]

Prayer

Prayer is an integral part of the Christian faith, so much so it deserves its own subheading. Prayer can be challenging for some autistic Christians if they find it hard to communicate with a God they cannot see. Father Matthew Schneider, an autistic Catholic priest, has written about prayer from his perspective: 'When autistics pray, we can go deep. However, autistic prayer is slightly different from neurotypical prayer.'[28] If an autistic person wants to establish a prayer life, it is important they find a way of praying that works for them, rather than forcing themselves into a way of communicating with God that they cannot relate to. I like the ACTS model of prayer which many of us learned in Sunday school – adoration, confession, thanksgiving and supplication. Having a formula like this can be helpful for autistic people who struggle with spontaneity, as it gives a framework to follow when you have no idea what to say.

Adoration

Adoration is when the believer praises God and considers his attributes: 'Great is the LORD and most worthy of praise; his greatness no one can fathom' (Psalm 145:3). Humans have a natural desire to praise things we like. Even if an autistic person struggles to conceptualise God, they can still praise God and feel a sense of awe and wonder by engaging with God's creation.

Confession

Whenever a Christian prays, they confess their sins and brokenness before God and seek his forgiveness: 'If we confess our sins, he is faithful and just to forgive us our sins and to cleanse us from all unrighteousness' (1 John 1:9). Repentance is an action: it involves turning away from sin and committing to live differently. Autistic people are just as prone to sin as anyone else, and it is important to own up when we mess up and commit to doing better next time.

Thanksgiving

Thanksgiving is mentioned one hundred and fourteen times in the Bible! We thank God for the blessings he has given us: 'always giving thanks to God the Father for everything, in the name of our Lord Jesus Christ' (Ephesians 5:20). Much has been written by psychologists regarding the benefits of gratitude for improving mental health. It's a good idea to regularly list the things you are grateful for in life.

Supplication

Supplicatory prayer is subdivided into petition, prayers for oneself, and intercession, prayers for others. Christians believe God is all-powerful and able to answer our requests: 'If you abide in me, and my words abide in you, ask whatever you wish, and it will be done for you' (John 15:7). 1 John 5:15 offers further clarification on this point: God is not a fairy godmother, rather prayers will be answered only 'according to his will'. However, as agents of God's love in the world, there must be a practical element to our prayers for others. As well as offering thoughts and prayers to an ill relative, why not ask how you can help them? The most powerful prayers should combine both words and action. To quote St Ignatius, 'Pray as if everything depended on God and work as if everything depended on you.'

Overall, I find this model of prayer simple and effective, even when I feel far from God. Prayers that are practical in focus can help people who feel too constrained by the language of traditional Christian prayer. Of course, there is no one correct way to pray. Every person deserves to find the method that allows them to connect with God.

The Bible and Doubt

It can be demoralising to be a Christian who has difficulty feeling an intimate connection to God, autistic or not. Western Christianity tends to be quite individualistic, emphasising the personal relationship between each believer and God, whereas the Bible is more focussed on how *communities* relate to God: 'so in Christ we, though many, form one body, and each member belongs to all the others' (Romans 12:5). There are plenty of Biblical authors who felt far from God but were able to stay true to the faith. The Book of Psalms is a good place to start; the authors are willing to express their most vulnerable emotions, no holds barred. Psalm 77 is the cry of someone at rock bottom, feeling utterly abandoned by God:

> Will the Lord reject forever?
> Will he never show his favour again?
>
> Has his unfailing love vanished forever?
> Has his promise failed for all time?
>
> Has God forgotten to be merciful?
> Has he in anger withheld his compassion? (vv. 7–9)

I'm sure we've all felt like this at times. We shouldn't shy away from expressing such sentiments – just like the Corrymeela Bible study I mentioned earlier, the church should be a community in which Christians feel able to talk about the highs and lows of their faith without facing judgement or condemnation. One of my favourite Bible verses is Mark 9:24, spoken by a man whose son was possessed: 'Lord, I believe! Help my unbelief!' This paradoxical statement could be the motto of my life! Knowing that a man who physically interacted with Jesus and witnessed his miracles still struggled with unbelief makes my own faith struggles seem more reasonable.

I will finish this chapter by emphasising what I said at the beginning: not all autistic people struggle to have a personal relationship with God, but many do. This chapter is aimed at the subset of autistic people who feel alienated by certain Christian teaching regarding how we relate to God. Sometimes, new ways of looking at timeless truths are necessary. As an autistic Christian, I have a deep desire to be part of something beyond myself, to follow the teachings of Jesus and establish the Kingdom of God on earth. I may not be able to communicate with an anthropomorphised God, but this I know: God is love, and autistic people are just as capable of giving and receiving love as anyone else. Many autistic adults face a life of isolation and misunderstanding; churches can offer a community of inclusive love for such individuals.

Questions for Reflection

- How do you relate to God?
- Do you ever feel different compared to other Christians?
- How do you pray?
- What helps you when you feel far from God?

CHAPTER 4

The Spirituality of Autism

Spirituality means different things to different people. In the broadest sense, spirituality involves being connected to something much larger than yourself, something that gives you a sense of meaning. For Christians, our spirituality centres around God, revealed through Jesus Christ. Christians are instructed to 'love the Lord your God with all your heart, and with all your soul, and with all your mind, and with all your strength' (Mark 12:30–31). This verse originated as part of the Jewish Shema in Deuteronomy and is then repeated by Jesus in three out of the four Gospels, so it's a pretty big deal. It raises some interesting questions with regards to autism: how can you love God 'with all your mind' when your mind works differently? Everyone relates to God in their own unique way, and no two Christians are exactly alike in their approach to spirituality. With that in mind, this chapter will explore some of the ways in which autistic Christians experience spirituality.

Autistic Love

Christianity and love go together like tea and biscuits. Neither one is complete without the other. Love is mentioned approximately five hundred times in the Bible and is an integral part of the very nature of God: 'God is love, and all who live in love live in God, and God lives in them' (1 John 4:7). But what is love? We certainly talk about it a lot, but we rarely stop to think exactly what love means. Anyone who studied theology and didn't fall asleep during Koine Greek class can tell you there are four types of love mentioned in the New Testament: *eros* (sexual), *philia* (friendship), *storge* (familial), and *agape* (unconditional, self-sacrificial). It's the latter that is most applicable to God. In the words of Martin Luther King Jr, 'Agape is something of the understanding, creative, redemptive goodwill for all men... It's what theologians would call the love of God working in the lives of men.'[29] An important thing to acknowledge about this kind of love is that it is an *action*, not a *feeling*. Jesus even tells us to love our enemies – that's certainly not the result of fuzzy feelings! We must act in a loving way towards others in our everyday lives, and it is through such actions that we can experience God. Connection is a vital part of spirituality, be it connection with God, nature, other people, or all of the above. To get even more theological, we are made in the image of an inherently connected and relational God. The Father, Son and Holy Spirit form a loving unit that Richard Rohr aptly calls 'the divine dance', and therefore we should aim to live out the trinitarian love of God through our practical love for fellow divine image-bearers.[30]

However, all this talk of love and connection is easier said than done for autistic people; the National Autistic Society reports that autistic people are seven times more likely to feel isolated compared to the general community.[31] A mother once told me that a youth leader had told her autistic son to relate to God in the same way that he relates to a best friend – except, her son had never had a best friend. He'd never had any friends. The metaphor was lost on him. I had a similar experience as a young Christian, when I was desperately lonely and yearning for connection. My favourite Bible verse was the words of Jesus in John 15:15: 'I no longer call you servants, because a servant does not know his master's business. Instead, I have called you friends, for everything that I learned from my Father I have made known to you.' I loved the idea of Jesus relating to his disciples as friends, as it spoke to a void in my life that needed to be filled. I didn't truly understand the impact of this verse until I began to experience connection with other people. I learned that a friend is someone who enjoys your company and sticks by you even at your worst – what a wonderful way to understand the love of God!

The idea that autistic people are unable to form meaningful relationships with other people is a myth, although it is true that we express our love in different ways. Even if they don't say much, the very fact that an autistic person wants to spend time with you means a lot. Likewise for going to church – if an autistic person is willing to bear the potential sensory and social discomfort of church, it shows how much they care about their faith, even if they do not say it outright.

David Delgado, an autistic Christian, has written about a couple who would always talk to him at church. At first he barely responded to them, but they didn't take it personally and kept on including him – nothing too overwhelming, just questions like 'how are you today?' or 'did you like the service?' Eventually, he felt comfortable enough to engage with them, and he now considers them friends. Delgado also encourages people to find out about his special interests as a means of connecting: 'Odds are the person probably has a subject they're extremely passionate about, so engage for a while. I have put Katie through hours of conversation about video games. She isn't a fan, but she listens and then says she doesn't really get it, but she's glad I'm excited, and then we move on.'[32] Such interactions have a spiritual impact, no matter how mundane they may seem – it helps autistic people feel included in the Kingdom of God.

Spirituality Beyond Words

What about those who cannot speak? Statistics are constantly changing, but the latest UK figures suggest that 30% of autistic people are non-verbal.[33] These people are not going to be able to participate in church activities in a conventional way, but that doesn't mean they can't experience spirituality. In academic discussions of autism, the phrase 'presuming competence' crops up a lot. This is the idea that we should presume non-verbal people can understand what is going on around them. In practice, this means talking to them and including them, even if you are not sure that they are listening. Non-verbal does not mean non-communicative. There are many ways to communicate beyond words, such as facial expressions, gestures and augmentative and alternative communication devices (AAC). Much of religious experience is ineffable, meaning it cannot be adequately described within the limitations of human language, even for neurotypical people. The Apostle Paul experienced this: 'the Spirit helps us in our weakness. We do not know what we ought to pray for, but the Spirit himself intercedes for us through wordless groans' (Romans 8:26). Non-verbal people have a vivid inner world that outsiders can only catch glimpses of, but they are fully known to God. I came across a really interesting article written by Ingela Visuri, a PhD student at Gävle University in Sweden, in which she explained that prayer can be especially meaningful for non-verbal autistic people as it enables them to communicate without relying on language or adhering to social protocols.[34] When praying, we should be able to express our inner thoughts and feelings without worrying about body language, facial expressions or taking turns. The believer is free to 'pray in the Spirit on all occasions with all kinds of prayers and requests' (Ephesians 6:8).

We also need to consider the spirituality of autistic people with intellectual disabilities, as approximately 40% of autistic people have some form of learning disability.[35] While I was studying at Queen's University Belfast I had the privilege of meeting Dr Jill Harshaw, a lecturer of Practical Theology who specialises in the spirituality of individuals with profound intellectual disability, including profound autism. She believes that our inclination to over-intellectualise faith does these individuals a disservice.[36] If salvation is conditional upon the person being able to understand doctrines like penal substitutionary atonement, this excludes people with intellectual disability. We need to rediscover the value of more contemplative theologies, such as those currently being popularised by Richard Rohr. Spiritual practices like Centring Prayer may be helpful for those with intellectual disability, as it focuses purely on *being* in the presence of God's love. Rohr describes it well: 'It is not about achieving anything, whether emptying your mind or finding peace or achieving a spiritual experience. There is no way to succeed at Centring Prayer, except to return again and again to love.'[37]

For Harshaw, academic work has a very personal dimension – her daughter Rebecca is non-verbal. She believes that her daughter and others with complex needs have a prophetic voice that can be expressed without speech. To prophesy, in the Biblical sense, does not mean predicting the future. Rather, it refers to someone who is appointed by God to remind others of timeless truths, just like the prophet Amos and his concern with justice for the oppressed. God often selects those who are looked down upon by the rest of society: 'The Lord does not look at the things people look at. People look at the outward appearance, but the Lord looks at the heart' (1 Samuel 16:7). Harshaw gives some examples of how her daughter teaches her about God's love. Rebecca teaches her that a person's worth is not defined by their health, independence or economic productivity – their worth is intrinsic by virtue of being human. She also teaches about the importance of being true to yourself. People with intellectual disabilities do not scheme, manipulate and lie like the rest of us. When she's happy, she shows it. When she's sad, she shows it. She accepts help and care without feeling embarrassed or ashamed. Harshaw describes caring for her daughter as a gift rather than a burden, taking to heart Jesus' teaching that it is better to give than to receive. As for her daughter's inner spirituality, Harshaw is sure that Rebecca has a mysterious connection to God:

> For a long time now I have been considering how Rebecca inhabits her capacity for relationship. What is her 'language of love?' As yet I have no definitive answers. But I know that, despite her lack of words, it is there. What goes on between Rebecca and God – her salvation – is not something I have language for. Yet, as she is undoubtedly a person loved into being by Him can I, can anyone doubt that, in some mysterious way, she knows and lives in relationship with the One who is love?[38]

Beware of Legalism

It is also important to be aware of what could go wrong when autistic people explore matters of religion and spirituality. One challenge quite a lot of autistic people face is taking quite a legalistic approach to Christianity, which is something I personally struggled with as a teenager. Such an approach can make Christianity and church seem like a never-ending list of demands and obligations rather than something lifegiving. Lamar Hardwick recognises this tendency in the way he approaches his faith. There are times he obsesses over the rules and rituals of faith, describing himself as 'a prime candidate for becoming extremely religious'.[39] If this is not dealt with appropriately, it can quickly morph into scrupulosity, a form of obsessive-compulsive disorder that causes a pathological level of religious guilt. Alex Lowry, an autistic Christian, has described his experience with scrupulosity:

> I struggled to pray for a long time and again this made me feel like I couldn't be a Christian. I would also obsess over whether I thought about God enough. I thought I had to think about God every second of the day. If I thought about something else I would have really negative thoughts about not being a Christian. I also felt I wasn't sorry enough for my sins, I would continually keep going over this in my head. I have realised that this is part of my autism and I must learn to not get stuck in such unhelpful thinking.[40]

What can you do if you or an autistic person you love is struggling in this way? At the risk of sounding extremely cliché, helping them to realise that they're not alone in their struggles can help. They may think the reason why they feel so much guilt is that they are a terrible, irredeemable person, but realising that lots of autistic people feel this way helps to contextualise things. If you are helping an autistic person with their faith, make sure to emphasise things like grace, forgiveness and freedom in Christ, not just a list of dos and don'ts. For instance, statements such as 'you *must* read the Bible and pray every day' may be perceived as too demanding. Better phrasing involves giving the person agency over the task and the option to refuse: 'If you think it would help you to engage more with God, try praying.' If the problem persists, it would be worthwhile seeking mental health treatment – for me, having counselling with someone who really understood scrupulosity made the obsessive aspect of autism much easier to deal with, which in turn helped me to relate to Christianity in a much healthier way.

Autism and Spiritual Leadership

So far we have mostly considered how churches can help autistic laypeople – what about autistic people in the pulpit? God calls people of all neurotypes to ministry. Plenty of spiritual leaders in the Bible had trouble speaking fluently. In the Old Testament, Moses describes himself as 'slow of speech and tongue' (Exodus 4:10) and in the New Testament, the Apostle Paul admits to being 'unskilled as a speaker' (2 Corinthians 11:6). Does this mean that Moses and Paul had autism? Perhaps, but it is impossible to retrospectively diagnose literary figures. Doing so could be considered *eisegesis*, reading things into the text that aren't there. Regardless of their exact diagnosis, both of these leaders were used by God to achieve great things even though they were not naturally charismatic. The same is true for autistic Christians today.

Father Matthew Schneider is an excellent example of an autistic clergyperson who is making a real difference.[41] He is a Catholic priest from the USA who didn't get diagnosed as autistic until he had been in ministry for a few years. He started off as a school chaplain, but he found it difficult to interact with the kids socially. He now considers this low point in his career to be a blessing in disguise, as it was the catalyst for his diagnosis. After finding out he was autistic, Schneider was able to work out what his strengths were and thus avoid being put into a ministry he was ill-equipped for. He now sees autistic people as his 'mission field', and he is keen to make the teachings and sacraments of his church accessible to all. He even has a very snazzy clerical shirt with 'Autistic Catholic' emblazoned on it! He hopes to eventually become a seminary lecturer, as the academic side of theology suits his very logical way of thinking.

The most important takeaway from Father Schneider's story is the importance of finding a ministry that is suited to the individual's calling. Ministry is not limited to the parish and autistic Christians shouldn't be discouraged if traditional forms of ministry are not suited to them. There's such a variety out there – clergy and Christian laypeople can be found providing spiritual support in schools, universities, prisons, hospitals, hospices and even airports (shoutout to the very nice airport chaplain I met in Schiphol). Additionally, the pandemic reminded us of the importance of digital ministry. Autistic people who are uncomfortable with in-person gatherings may be able to fulfil their spiritual calling through blogging and other forms of online ministry. While I was at theological college, I volunteered for a Christian charity that supports merchant seafarers. It was certainly an obscure ministry, but one I enjoyed very much. It involved working with a subset of people who work in very isolated environments for most of the year. My experience of feeling isolated from the rest of the world made it all the more meaningful when I had the opportunity to offer these people some much needed social interaction, even if it was brief. In many ways, I felt like I had found my niche. I hope and pray that all autistic Christians will be able to find their niche.

Questions for Reflection

- What does spirituality mean to you?
- What gives you a sense of meaning?
- Have you ever taken a legalistic approach to religion?
- Do you feel called to ministry? If so, in what way?

Conclusion

Congratulations, you have reached the end of these autistic Christian ramblings. The fact that you have taken the time to read this booklet demonstrates you care deeply about welcoming autistic people into Christian communities. Thank you! There's been a lot of information, so here's a handy summary of what we've covered:

Chapter 1 – Defining Autism

Autism is a spectrum condition, meaning each person will present differently. There are a few traits that almost all autistic people have: social difficulties, sensory hypersensitivity and intense interests. Beyond these, each autistic person is unique. You've probably heard the phrase 'If you've met one person with autism, you've met one person with autism' – it's true! That's why it's so important to understand each individual's strengths and weaknesses. At the end of the chapter, I listed some of my autistic role models – I would encourage you to do your own research and find some role models of your own.

Chapter 2 – **Autism and the Church**

Approximately 1 in 100 people are autistic, a statistic that will likely increase as diagnostic services improve. It's probable that each congregation has at least one autistic member, and the church needs to be equipped to welcome them. There are plenty of Bible passages that discuss inclusion in the church: 1 Corinthians 12 compares the church to a human body, where each part has a unique role and no one part is better than the others, and Luke 14 contains the Parable of the Great Banquet, in which the Kingdom of God is compared to a party where 'the poor, the crippled, the blind and the lame' have a place at the table. A list of practical suggestions is given to help you bring this parable to life in your own church.

Chapter 3 – **Autism and God**

Autistic people think differently, therefore it makes sense that the way we think about God might be different than most. God doesn't change, but the way in which humans interact with him does. Chapter three summarises some of the latest research on autism and religion, including the interesting link between autism and atheism. This doesn't mean all autistic people find it difficult to believe in God – it just means they're more likely to struggle with doubt compared to neurotypicals. I then considered how autistic people can relate to key aspects of the faith, such as prayer and scripture.

Chapter 4 – **The Spirituality of Autism**

Chapter four considers different ways in which autistic people can be 'spiritual'. Christians are instructed to 'love the Lord your God with all your heart, and with all your soul, and with all your mind, and with all your strength'.

If autistic people love God 'with all their mind', it may look different to love expressed by a neurotypical mind. This is especially the case for non-verbal people who will express love in their own unique way. Furthermore, autism should not preclude someone from church leadership if they feel called to a position of spiritual authority – there are many autistic priests/pastors, people like Lamar Hardwick and Matthew Schneider who are a great encouragement to autistic Christians.

Christianity offers wholeness to those who are broken. Autistic people can turn to Christ for forgiveness and unconditional love, and they can come to the church – the body of Christ – for a welcoming community. One of the people I interviewed put it this way: 'Being in church makes me feel part of a loving community, so very different from the mess and hate of the world.'[42] I experienced such a community recently during a trip abroad – I attended an international church made up of people of many different nationalities and backgrounds, a place where I felt welcomed despite never having set foot in that city before. There were other neurodiverse people there, including a man with Down Syndrome who felt free to make joyful noises throughout the service. It was a wonderful example of the Kingdom of God on earth.

Let this booklet be a call to action – what can you personally do to support your autistic brothers and sisters in Christ? It can be something as simple as providing earplugs in church, or making an effort to include someone who rarely talks. Remember, Jesus said 'whatever you did for one of the least of these... you did for me' (Matthew 25:40). In a world of isolation and rejection, autistic people often feel like they are 'the least of these'.

To finish, I will try to sum up the essence of my faith. It's hard for me to express precisely what I believe. I can't summarise it neatly into 95 theses or 39 articles, but this I know:

I am an autistic Christian.

I love God.

Even if I struggle to relate to God on a personal level, I can experience God's love through connection with other image-bearers.

I love Jesus.

By reading about the life and teachings of Jesus, I can understand what it means to live a Godly life, even to the point of laying down your life for others.

I love the church.

The church is a foretaste of the Kingdom of God, a place where broken people can find wholeness.

I hope and pray that more autistic people can experience church community like I have.

Amen.

Endnotes

1. *National Health Service.* 'What is Autism?'. 18 April 2022. Available at: https://www.nhs.uk/conditions/autism/what-is-autism/.
2. Temple Grandin, *Different ... Not Less: Inspiring Stories of Achievement and Successful Employment from Adults with Autism, Asperger's, and ADHD* (Arlington: Future Horizons, 2012).
3. See Stephen Shore, *Beyond the Wall: Personal Experiences with Autism and Asperger Syndrome* (Shawnee Mission: Autism Asperger Publishing Co. 2003).
4. Hans Christian Andersen, *The Fairy Tale of my Life* (London: Paddington Press, 1871).
5. Michael Fitzgerald, *Autism and Creativity: Is There a Link between Autism in Men and Exceptional Ability?* (Abingdon: Routledge, 2004), p. 28.
6. *Department of Health.* 'The Prevalence of Autism (including Asperger's Syndrome) in School Age Children in Northern Ireland'. 20 May 2021. Available at: https://www.health-ni.gov.uk/publications/prevalence-autism-including-aspergers-syndrome-school-age-children-northern-ireland-2021.
7. See Lorcan Kenny, et al., 'Which terms should be used to describe autism? Perspectives from the UK autism community', *Autism*, Vol. 20, Issue 4 (2016): 442–462.

8 Eileen Lamb, 'Is Autism a Superpower?', *The Autism Café*, 22 November 2020. Available at: https://theautismcafe.com/autism-a-superpower/.

9 Ron Sandison, 'An Interview With Lamar Hardwick, The Autism Pastor', *The Art of Autism*. 22 October 2021. Available at: https://the-art-of-autism.com/an-interview-with-lamar-hardwick-the-autism-pastor/.

10 Lamar Hardwick, *I Am Strong: The Life and Journey of an Autistic Pastor* (Little Elm: eLectio Publishing, 2017), and *Disability and the Church: A Vision for Diversity and Inclusion* (Westmont: Inter-Varsity Press, 2021).

11 *BBC Newsbeat*. 'I'm A Celeb's Anne Hegerty opens up about Asperger's'. 20 November 2018. Available at: https://www.bbc.co.uk/news/newsbeat-46272608.

12 *National Autistic Society*. 'What is Autism?'. Available at: https://www.autism.org.uk/advice-and-guidance/what-is-autism.

13 UK Parliament. 'Autism – Overview of Policy and Services', *House of Commons Library*. 1 February 2022. Available at: https://commonslibrary.parliament.uk/research-briefings/cbp-7172/.

14 Hardwick, *I Am Strong*, p. 90.

15 Private conversation with author. Quoted with permission.

16 Private conversation with author. Quoted with permission.

17 Amy Fenton Lee, *Leading a Special Needs Ministry* (Nashville: B&H Publishing Group, 2013).

18 Grant Macaskill, *Autism and the Church* (Waco: Baylor University Press, 2019).

19 Matthew Hutson, 'Does Autism Lead to Atheism?', *Psychology Today*. 30 May 2012. Available at: https://www.psychologytoday.com/gb/blog/psyched/201205/does-autism-lead-atheism.

20 Catherine Caldwell-Harris, et al., 'Religious Belief Systems of Persons with High Functioning Autism', *Proceedings of the Annual Meeting of the Cognitive Science Society*, 33 (2011): 3362–3366.

21 Ara Norenzayan, Will M. Gervais, and Kali H. Trzesniewski, 'Mentalizing Deficits Constrain Belief in a Personal God', *PLOS ONE*, Vol. 7, Issue 5 (2012). Available at: https://journals.plos.org/plosone/article?id=10.1371/journal.pone.0036880.

[22] Hutson, 'Does Autism Lead to Atheism'.

[23] Bethany T. Heywood, and Jesse M. Bering, 'Meant to be: how religious beliefs and cultural religiosity affect the implicit bias to think teleologically', *Religion, Brain and Behaviour*, Vol. 4, Issue 3 (2014): 183–201.

[24] Karen Schrock, 'People with Asperger's less likely to see purpose behind the events in their lives', *Scientific American*, 29 May 2010. Available at: https://blogs.scientificamerican.com/observations/people-with-aspergers-less-likely-to-see-purpose-behind-the-events-in-their-lives/.

[25] Preston Sprinkle, 'Is Jesus My Boyfriend?', *Theology in the Raw*. 24 February 2015. Available at: https://theologyintheraw.com/blog/2015/02/is-jesus-my-boyfriend/.

[26] John Shelby Spong [@JohnSelbySpong] in a tweet published 20 April 2015. *Twitter*. Available at: https://twitter.com/johnshelbyspong/status/589940429845504000.

[27] Richard Holloway, *Doubts and Loves: What is Left of Christianity* (Edinburgh: Cannongate, 2001), p. 174.

[28] Fr. Matthew P. Schneider, 'Deep Autistic Prayer: A Personal Prayer Beyond Words'. 20 September 2019. *Through Catholic Lenses*. Available at: https://www.patheos.com/blogs/throughcatholiclenses/2019/09/prayer-beyond-words-for-autistics/.

[29] Martin Luther King, '"Loving Your Enemies": Sermon Delivered at Dexter Avenue Baptist Church', *The Martin Luther King, Jr. Research and Education Institute, Stanford University*. Sermon delivered: 17 November 1957. Available at: https://kinginstitute.stanford.edu/king-papers/documents/loving-your-enemies-sermon-delivered-dexter-avenue-baptist-church.

[30] Richard Rohr, *The Divine Dance: The Trinity And Your Transformation* (London: SPCK, 2016).

[31] *National Autistic Society*. 'Left Stranded: Our New Report into the Impact of Coronavirus'. Published: 7 September 2020. Available at: https://www.autism.org.uk/what-we-do/news/coronavirus-report.

[32] David Delgado, 'Doing Church with Autism Spectrum Disorder'. *The Gospel Coalition*. Published: 10 July 2019. Available at:

https://www.thegospelcoalition.org/article/church-autism-spectrum-disorder/.

[33] Kimberly Holland, 'Understanding Nonspeaking Autism', *healthline*. Updated: 1 November 2021. Available at: https://www.healthline.com/health/autism/nonverbal-autism.

[34] Ingela Visuri, 'Rethinking Autism, Theism, and Atheism: Bodiless Agents and Imaginary Realities', *Archive for the Psychology of Religion*, Vol. 4, Issue 1 (2018): 1–31.

[35] *Autistica*. 'Learning Disability and Autism'. Available at: https://www.autistica.org.uk/what-is-autism/signs-and-symptoms/learning-disability-and-autism.

[36] Jill Harshaw, *God Beyond Words: Christian Theology and the Spiritual Experiences of People with Profound Intellectual Disabilities* (London: Jessica Kingsley Publishers, 2016).

[37] Richard Rohr, 'Love: Week 1 Summary'. Daily Meditation for 2 January 2016, *Center for Action and Contemplation*. Available at: https://cac.org/love-week-1-summary-2016-01-02/.

[38] Jill Harshaw, 'Autism and Love – A response to "Autism and Love, Learning What Love Looks Like" by Professor John Swinton', *Practical Theology*, Vol. 5, Issue 3 (2012): 285.

[39] Hardwick, *I Am Strong*, p. 114.

[40] Alex Lowery, 'Autistic and Christian', *evangelicals now*. August 2015. Available at: https://www.e-n.org.uk/2015/08/features/autistic-and-christian/8dd8b/.

[41] Ron Sandison, 'Father Matthew Schneider Navigating Life As Priest On The Autism Spectrum', *The Art of Autism*. 13 August 2021. Available at: https://the-art-of-autism.com/father-matthew-schneider-navigating-life-as-priest-on-the-autism-spectrum/.

[42] Private conversation with author. Quoted with permission.

Bibliography and Further Reading

Andersen, Hans Christian, *The Fairy Tale of my Life* (London: Paddington Press, 1871).

Autistica [website]. 'Learning Disability and Autism'. Available at: https://www.autistica.org.uk/what-is-autism/signs-and-symptoms/learning-disability-and-autism. Last accessed: 4 April 2022.

BBC Newsbeat [website]. 'I'm A Celeb's Anne Hegerty opens up about Asperger's'. Published: 20 November 2018. Available at: https://www.bbc.co.uk/news/newsbeat-46272608. Last accessed: 4 April 2022.

Caldwell-Harris, Catherine, et al. 'Religious Belief Systems of Persons with High Functioning Autism', *Proceedings of the Annual Meeting of the Cognitive Science Society*, 33 (2011): 3362–3366.

Delgado, David, 'Doing Church with Autism Spectrum Disorder', *The Gospel Coalition* [website]. Published: 10 July 2019. Available at: https://www.thegospelcoalition.org/article/church-autism-spectrum-disorder/. Last accessed: 4 April 2022.

Department of Health [website]. 'The Prevalence of Autism (including Asperger's Syndrome) in School Age Children in Northern Ireland'. Published: 20 May 2021. Available at: https://www.health-ni.gov.uk/publications/prevalence-autism-including-aspergers-syndrome-school-age-children-northern-ireland-2021. Last accessed: 4 April 2022.

Fitzgerald, Michael, *Autism and Creativity: Is There a Link between Autism in Men and Exceptional Ability?* (Abingdon: Routledge, 2004).

Grandin, Temple, *Different … Not Less: Inspiring Stories of Achievement and Successful Employment from Adults with Autism, Asperger's, and ADHD* (Arlington: Future Horizons, 2012).

Hardwick, Lamar, *I Am Strong: The Life and Journey of an Autistic Pastor* (Little Elm: eLectio Publishing, 2017).

_____. *Disability and the Church: A Vision for Diversity and Inclusion* (Westmont: Inter-Varsity Press, 2021).

Harshaw, Jill, 'Autism and Love – A response to "Autism and Love, Learning What Love Looks Like" by Professor John Swinton', *Practical Theology*, Vol. 5, Issue 3 (2012): 279–286.

_____. *God Beyond Words: Christian Theology and the Spiritual Experiences of People with Profound Intellectual Disabilities* (London: Jessica Kingsley, 2016).

Heywood, Bethany T. and Bering, Jesse M., 'Meant to be: how religious beliefs and cultural religiosity affect the implicit bias to think teleologically', *Religion, Brain and Behaviour*, Vol. 4, Issue 3 (2014): 183–201.

Holland, Kimberly, 'Understanding Nonspeaking Autism', *healthline* [website]. Updated: 1 November 2021. Available at: https://www.healthline.com/health/autism/nonverbal-autism. Last accessed: 4 April 2022.

Holloway, Richard, *Doubts and Loves: What is Left of Christianity* (Edinburgh: Cannongate, 2001).

Hutson, Matthew. 'Does Autism Lead to Atheism?'
Psychology Today. Published: 30 May 2012. Available
at: https://www.psychologytoday.com/gb/blog/
psyched/201205/does-autism-lead-atheism. Last
accessed: 4 April 2022.

Kenny, Lorcan, et al. 'Which terms should be used to
describe autism? Perspectives from the UK autism
community', *Autism*, Vol. 20, Issue 4 (2016): 442–462.

King, Martin Luther, '"Loving Your Enemies": Sermon
Delivered at Dexter Avenue Baptist Church', *The Martin
Luther King, Jr. Research and Education Institute,
Stanford University* [website]. Sermon delivered: 17
November 1957. Available at: https://kinginstitute.
stanford.edu/king-papers/documents/loving-your-
enemies-sermon-delivered-dexter-avenue-baptist-
church. Last accessed: 4 April 2022.

Lamb, Eileen, 'Is Autism a Superpower?', *The Autism Café*
[website]. Published: 22 November 2020. Available at:
https://theautismcafe.com/autism-a-superpower/. Last
accessed: 4 April 2022.

Lee, Amy Fenton, *Leading a Special Needs Ministry*
(Nashville: B&H Publishing Group, 2013).

Lowery, Alex, 'Autistic and Christian', *evangelicals now*
[website]. August 2015. Available at: https://www.e-n.
org.uk/2015/08/features/autistic-and-christian/8dd8b/.
Last accessed: 4 April 2022.

Macaskill, Grant, *Autism and the Church* (Waco: Baylor
University Press, 2019)

National Autistic Society [website]. 'Left Stranded: Our New
Report into the Impact of Coronavirus'. Published: 7
September 2020. Available at: https://www.autism.org.
uk/what-we-do/news/coronavirus-report. Last accessed:
4 April 2022.

_____. 'What is Autism?'. Available at: https://www.autism.org.uk/advice-and-guidance/what-is-autism. Last accessed: 4 April 2022.

National Health Service [website]. 'What is Autism?'. Published: 18 April 2022. Available at: https://www.nhs.uk/conditions/autism/what-is-autism/. Last accessed: 4 April 2022.

Norenzayan, Ara, Gervais, Will M., and Trzesniewski, Kali H., 'Mentalizing Deficits Constrain Belief in a Personal God', *PLOS ONE*, Vol. 7, Issue 5 (2012). Available at: https://journals.plos.org/plosone/article?id=10.1371/journal.pone.0036880. Last accessed: 4 April 2022.

Rohr, Richard, 'Love: Week 1 Summary' (Daily Meditation for 2 January 2016). *Center for Action and Contemplation* [website]. Available at: https://cac.org/love-week-1-summary-2016-01-02/. Last accessed: 4 April 2022.

_____. *The Divine Dance: The Trinity And Your Transformation* (London: SPCK, 2016).

Sandison, Ron, 'An Interview With Lamar Hardwick, The Autism Pastor'. Published: 22 October 2020. *The Art of Autism* [website]. Available at: https://the-art-of-autism.com/an-interview-with-lamar-hardwick-the-autism-pastor/. Last accessed: 4 April 2022.

_____. 'Father Matthew Schneider Navigating Life As Priest On The Autism Spectrum', *The Art of Autism* [website]. Published: 13 August 2021. Available at: https://the-art-of-autism.com/father-matthew-schneider-navigating-life-as-priest-on-the-autism-spectrum/. Last accessed: 4 April 2022.

Schneider, Fr. Matthew P., 'Deep Autistic Prayer: A Personal Prayer Beyond Words'. Published: 20 September 2019. *Through Catholic Lenses* [website]. Available at: https://www.patheos.com/blogs/throughcatholiclenses/2019/09/prayer-beyond-words-for-autistics/. Last accessed: 4 April 2022.

Schrock, Karen, 'People with Asperger's less likely to see purpose behind the events in their lives.' *Scientific American*. Published: 29 May 2010. Available at: https://blogs.scientificamerican.com/observations/people-with-aspergers-less-likely-to-see-purpose-behind-the-events-in-their-lives/. Last accessed: 4 April 2022.

Shore, Stephen, *Beyond the Wall: Personal Experiences with Autism and Asperger Syndrome* (Shawnee Mission: Autism Asperger Publishing Co., 2003).

Spong, John Shelby [@JohnSelbySpong], 'God is not a noun, that demands to be defined, God is a verb that invites us to live, to love and to be.' *Twitter*. Published: 20 April 2015 12:55 a.m. Available at: https://twitter.com/johnshelbyspong/status/589940429845504000. Last accessed: 4 April 2022.

Sprinkle, Preston, 'Is Jesus My Boyfriend?', *Theology in the Raw* [website]. 24 February 2015. Available at: https://theologyintheraw.com/blog/2015/02/is-jesus-my-boyfriend/. Last accessed: 4 April 2022.

UK Parliament. 'Autism – Overview of Policy and Services', *House of Commons Library* [website]. 1 February 2022. Available at: https://commonslibrary.parliament.uk/research-briefings/cbp-7172/. Last accessed: 4 April 2022.

Visuri, Ingela, 'Rethinking Autism, Theism, and Atheism: Bodiless Agents and Imaginary Realities', *Archive for the Psychology of Religion*, Vol. 40, Issue 1 (2018): 1–31.

About the Author

Erin Burnett was born and raised in Belfast, Northern Ireland. Her debut novel, *Liza's Avenger*, was published when she was still in school. She has a Theology degree from Queen's University and enjoys exploring the intersection between religion and contemporary social issues. She is currently studying for a Masters in Practical Theology at the University of Glasgow.

In addition to writing, Erin enjoys cycling and travelling. Of the 75 countries she has visited, her favourite is Japan.

erinburnettauthor.co.uk